After You

Patricia Osborne Malnati

the Peppertree Press
Sarasota, Florida

Copyright © Patricia Osborne Malnati, 2015

All rights reserved. Published by the Peppertree Press, LLC.
the Peppertree Press and associated logos are trademarks of
the Peppertree Press, LLC.

No part of this publication may be reproduced, stored in a retrieval
system, transmitted in any form or by any means, electronic, mechanical,
photocopying, recording, or otherwise, without prior written permission of
the publisher and author/illustrator. Graphic design by Rebecca Barbier.

For information regarding permission,
call 941-922-2662 or contact us at our website:
www.peppertreepublishing.com or write to:
the Peppertree Press, LLC.
Attention: Publisher
1269 First Street, Suite 7
Sarasota, Florida 34236

ISBN: 978-1-61493-355-7

Library of Congress Number: 2015905725

Printed May 2015

Dedication

Lisa
Tim
Keri
Amanda

In Appreciation

I feel this book in its entirety is from God whom I thank for this gift.
Also, Nettie Grace Brown, my agent.
Just like Rod McKuen, Tammy Wynette and George Jones would give you pause for loving words.

Table of Contents

SECTION ONE   1

After You 2
The Page We're On 3
Loving You 4
Please Stay 5
Let's Ride 6
As You Travel 8
Lessons in Love 10
Love Calls 11
Cold Weather 12
A Heart of Stone 13
To Be One with You 14
Broken and Tired 15
Love's Quest 16
Coming Back to You 17
Still, I will Love You 18
Love Is Patient 19
Time 20
Don't Forget 21
This Heart 22
Meet Me 23
Full Moon 24
A Lover's Song 25
Hello 26
For the Ride 27
Rough Seas 28

Your Eyes 29
Just Love Me 30
The Sunrise 31
Remember 32
That Smile 33
A Song for You 34
A Moment in Time 35
Chapter ? 36
An Old Flame 37
Chains 38
Life 39
Step Lightly on Leaving 40
These Loving Memories 42
Give Me One-Night Stands ... 43
Given Time 45
Real Life 46
Call Back 47
Sometimes 48
You Said What? 49
Evolving I 50
Wanting You or One Eighty ... 51
A Perfect Rose 52
Too Soon 54
There's Always Hope 56

SECTION TWO 59

Trying to Show an Inner Talent (or Getting Off the Subject).......... 58	Loss of a Child........................ 73
Please Be Dad......................... 60	The Hunter............................... 74
On Rod McKuen	The Prayer............................... 75
I Love Him 62	My Child................................... 76
Millie 64	No Longer................................ 77
Annette 65	Son 78
Nettie 66	This Sunny Morn 79
Lisa.. 67	On Miller Lites and Vantage Blues 80
Linda, My Friend...................... 68	Missing Pages of Life 81
Joy.. 69	Save the Rest!........................ 83
Another Empty Monday 70	Abused One............................. 85
Autumn 72	Bella... 86

SECTION THREE 87

Touch Me as You Tell Me........ 88	Nurses' Nightmares 93
If We Can, We Will, Friend 90	Home Health Nurses 94
A Lonely Man........................... 92	PPS 95

v

Section One

After You

I'm going to write a book
Someday
And name it after you

You could take a look
One day
Or maybe read it through.

The title
Centered carefully
The cover done
In blue.

The center pages
All left blank
Because there's
Nothing after you

The Page We're On

I could walk with you
on beaches
sit with you by mountain streams.

I could listen to
your heartaches
share with you your latest dreams.

We could both share life's
great pleasures
mellow slowly with the age

If you'd only read some new book,
or, slowly
gently turn the page.

Loving You

The words are still
unspoken
They lie timid
on the tongue

Like words to a
brand new love song
written
but as yet unsung

So walk with me
in friendship
warm me with your smile
stay with me

whenever you can
if only for a while
because I'm
loving you

Please Stay

You move aside now
hoping I'll find someone
or something
more fulfilling in my life.

Is That Possible?

You fill my whole world
with beauty
and love
just by opening the front door.

You empty it on leaving

In and out of my life
like a thought
passing through my mind
mostly thoughts of you.

Doors open
and close too easily
for you.

I need a new lock anyway.

I'll put it on the
outside!!!

Let's Ride

My heart's been running on empty
My life's been put on hold—
My emotions raw and blistered
Like a blast from winter's cold.

But time will be the healer
This season too will end
And hopefully as time goes by
You'll come to be my friend.

Your smile will be my sunshine
Your touch will be my fuel
Your love will take me places
Not learned about in school—

So gather up your trappings
Hold your breath and buckle in
We'll take a ride you'll not forget
And we'll take it again and again!

Sometimes

Sometimes your heart is torn
Between the right thing
And the wrong

Sometimes your life reminds
You of some old country song
Of broken hearts
And promises
And unfulfilled life's dreams

And one-night stands
And skirmishes
And unimportant schemes

But life is just
A pathway
A journey
To the shore

Where He will hold
You gently
And safely evermore

As You Travel

Put you two down
In Paris
And look what happens

No time for
Les Champs Elysees
We're on our way to
Germany
Send you a card
From there

Now leaving Verona
For Florence in the a.m.
Going on to Rome?
Hope you kissed
One French belly just to compare
If you kissed one in
Germany you won't make it to Rome!

Juliet would come
To life
for some things
like lovers wandering
not knowing of their end.

But
Rome was everything
Big Beautiful – Dirty
And Exciting

Can you still see
Naples and Sicily
And love all through the night

And when you come home
will things still
be right?

Tell me of traveling
and my heart will travel
with you
Wish you well
and guide you
through the many
twists and turns of
Foreign kisses
that fit just right
on this
one stormy night
here
        Home.

Lessons in Love

And You
the little cherub
out confusing lovers
twice your age

I think you had lessons
From someone
I know
or read the same book

You see
with age comes
some awareness of
people
Again you become unaware
of the games
in life
So you lose

As You Love

Games people play
Should have been
Printed as a handbook for lovers!

Love Calls

I sit quietly
Not wanting
Or needing to speak.

Your eyes in conversation
With my heart.

Words felt
But not spoken of
Such is love
These days.

Unexpected, needed
Quietly confusing the most
Innocent of Lovers.

Cold Weather

That day
you crawled up on my chest
and nestled in
Just like a newborn pup
needing that warmth
That beating heart.

Today, Nothing
my heart still beats
my body is still warm
But you don't need me
It's so cold!

If I could just see you
present myself to you
I know it would be different
for your need comes to
life in my presence
At least your need for me.

Even your absence
calls my heart

Cold dreary days
are good for all of us
They make the sunny days
so much brighter
and warmer.
Bring back that blanket
of love you gave me
It's going to be a
long winter.

A Heart of Stone

I walked along
the rocky shore
Thinking of love
and maybe more
I found a heart not broken yet
Saved it for you
Thought I'd let
you hold it for a while
yours was broken
mine is too
and so we'll just hold this one true
and share it
It's made of stone
It will not break. Just save it now
for old times' sake

you hold it for a while
I'll just enjoy your smile.

To Be One with You

To be one with you,
My Love,
to walk the same paths,
hand in hand.
To move always in the same direction
and even when divided or changing
to know of the coming together again.

To be one with you,
My Love,
to have our hearts swell,
our lips tell,
of the same dreams,
the same goals,
together as one.

But no
—STAY AWARE—
That can't be
for we came together in midstream
each flowing to our own ocean
but meeting here,
until the tides go out again.

Broken and Tired

And so you leave me
Broken and tired
my heart is broken
my mind is tired
from loving
You

You say
it's easy
NOT to feel
I say it's
easy
NOT to know
HOW!

One day
You'll know
just as I do
that loving you
is hard
When all that's easy passes by
within reach.

Love's Quest

My lips just brush your cheek
I sense the passion there within
As you pull back
I feel the warmth
Your breath
Upon my skin
My heart just whispers caution
Yet my arms
Reach out again
How sad to think
This quest for love
Could be in vain
Again

Coming Back to You

My heart will travel now
to old
and yet new places,
give it wisdom
let it settle
where warmth and love will shelter

Take my hand, love,
and know
its touch is weary
having caressed many a fool
yet
loving them just the same
but never knowing it would travel here
again

Old memories beautiful memories
of fun and laughter
of getting high and coming down again
of warm smiles and strong arms
holding me
and bringing me home to friends

Take this lonely heart now
and let yours
warm it with its breath
guide it with its truth
hold it with its strength
and show me how things could have been

And maybe
will be soon
if not forever
then just for a while

Still, I will Love You

Sometimes I run
On empty
No time
To fill 'er up
But love is
What it can be
Not always a full cup
So think of me
At daybreak
And Think of me
At dusk
Hold me close
Whenever you can
Just leave me
When you must

Love Is Patient

It's only gentle longing
You see within the stare
A quest for true belonging
Not another long affair

You deftly stir the passion
Lying deep within
Then turn away
You're safe today
You reined them in again

Those messages sent subtlety
Read only by a few
Not returned
They're resting here
And wait patiently for you

Time

We could stroll down
A country lane
Spread a blanket
By a stream

We could break
Some bread
Pour some wine
And let each other dream

Watch butterflies frolic
Aimlessly
The sun dancing
On your hair

If time
Would only let us be
What a moment we could share.

Don't Forget

We met in the fall
of life
And winter's coming soon
Let's swim in December
And skate thin ice
In June
I'll hold you every evening
Make love to you each dawn
Just, please,
Don't forget
To miss me when I'm gone.

This Heart

Take this heart
That's given you
And hold it in your hand

One day you'll
Look at love anew
And you will understand

That patience
And restraint are born
With time
And life's long learning

But really what
Has brought us here
Is two hearts gentle yearning
For love and real acceptance
No matter who we are
So step back now
And look again
In time
It's not so far

Meet Me

A suitcase full of heartache
A backpack full of sorrow
I'll meet you at the station
We'll leave them there tomorrow

We'll light out on a southbound train
Maybe visit all the beaches
Sunshine will be our wake-up call
We'll see what the moon might teach us

Full Moon

The evening
gone now.
Riding rolling thunder
into the night.

And only lightning
Lights
These avenues of loneliness
That you have left with me

But I can see.
The moon helps, full now.
It makes me think of you
And how you
Fill me.

A Lover's Song

I looked into your eyes today
And all that I could see
Were the deepest wells of loneliness
Looking back at me.

I tried to pass the emptiness
And push on through the tears
But you deflected my caress
You wouldn't let me near.

Hope someday, someone comes along
And you may let him in
If you could hear a lover's song
You'd never cry again.

Hello

Hello was all you said that day
And as you turned and walked away
I knew your voice had whispered to my soul.

Time has come, and time has gone
Yet still the memory lingers on
I never knew my heart would miss you so.

I hope to see you one more time
And hope your heart remembers mine
Cause my heart just won't seem to let you go.

For the Ride

I ride this moment of passion
full tilt
until
wilted, limp
You whisper my name
and
Without shame
I stand
once more
Proud
To be beside you
for a time
or inside you
for the climb—
of my life—

No other has ever
Sated
Like you
I hated—to leave.

Rough Seas

Even a Surfer
Off Australia's coast
Knows nothing of rough seas.

Till he rides the
Waves of loneliness
That you have left
With me.

Your Eyes

Your eyes tell me a story,
I hope no one else will read.
A story of a longing, a hunger and a need.

The longing is for someone
To come and follow through.
The hunger is for passion
And only passion will do.

The need is for a someone
Who cares enough to see
You'll settle for no less than
Someone with all three.

Just Love Me

Look at me heart
Loving you
Asking yours
To love me too.

Knowing you must
Walk away
Knowing you
Can never stay

But hearts have ways
All of their own
They don't like
To be alone

They reach out
And take the hands
Of love that's warm
And understands

So even if we
Ever part
You can smile
And know our hearts

Are walking on
Some beach somewhere
Holding hands
Without a care
And loving

Just love me

The Sunrise

Don't make me
A teardrop
In your river of sorrow

Let me be
Part of the sunrise
That brings you tomorrow

Part of the happiness
That fills your life
The part that's serenity
No part of the strife

So give me a smile
And we'll dance in the sun
Let's laugh for a while
And we'll always have fun

Remember

Take the time to know the feelings
Deep within my heart
Take the time to see the flame
Not just the fire start

Save the burning embers
They'll warm you in December
When all the world
Is locked down hard
With ice and snow
Remember
Me.

That Smile

An old flame
Can rekindle
Feelings left with time

A spark brought forth
By memories
Only yours and mine

A touch, a smile, a glance
Or maybe
Something in your eyes
Or hair I ran my
Fingers through
In younger years
Gone by

Whatever it may
Bring us
We'll try it for a while
I only hope
That if we part
You keep that
Same sweet smile
For Me

A Song for You

I'm going to write a song for you
And play it in the wind.
And it will blow across the miles
To touch your heart, my friend.

And when you hear the melody
That's playing in that tune
You'll only want to come to me
And hopefully, real soon.

So if you're looking out tonight
And see the branches swaying
You'll know it's my heart's song to you—
Your heart knows what it's saying.

A Moment in Time

If I could save one moment in time
I'd save a moment with you.

Cause above earthly pleasures,
But
Below the Divine,
There's a place that's special and new.

The friends that I've met
And lovers I've had
Are special in some little way,
But
You've hit a place
That's new in my heart,

You're beautiful!
That's all I can say.

Chapter ?

These words flow from
This used old pen
Like clay from a potter's wheel.

It's how I tell you
Who I am
And what I really feel.

If you can know
One man in life
And see the inside turning
You'll know that each
Forgotten wife
Is someone else's yearning.

And just like love
People never change
It'll go on through the ages.
You read one book
You put it down
Pick another up
And turn the pages.

An Old Flame

An old flame
May rekindle
But will it keep a fire?

Or is it just
An earthly need
Rising from desire?

Over time even
Rivers change
And flow to different tides
Sometimes we must
Test the waters
And even try the rides.

To love and
Be loved
Drives a man
More than he may know

Just launch your feelings
Honestly
Keep afloat and
Let them go.

GOOD LUCK

Chains

I come to you
Though fettered
By chains you cannot see.

My heart sings with
The passion
Your touch creates in me.

They come as cherished tidbits
Your fleeting looks,
Your smile.

They remind me of
Love's pleasures
I've not known
For quite some while.

Life

One touch
Can tell you
More than words
Could ever say
Life is short
Love is warm
And winter's
On the way

Step Lightly on Leaving

You walked across Vermont
that summer
and stirred the heart
of a restless stranger.

Some mountain breeze
must have whispered to me
of your nearness
or
was it that stream
that babbled on by the place
where I used to sit
and dream
of a love like yours

Could it have been
the roaring of that
raging river at the gorge
where I camped out that night
alone
I lay on my back
staring at the stars
and dreaming of a smile
as inviting
a body as exciting
as yours turned out to be

Now
our hearts race as one
as we meet on this common ground
foreign to us both
yet
home now
for the love we've shared
and will

Step lightly on leaving
my love
for my heart still trembles
with the wonder of it all.

These Loving Memories

That memory comes back now
your silhouette through the moonlight
falling on the water
sent my senses reeling,
your hand so deftly disrobed
my very being
letting fall on the sand
more than just my clothing
to be washed away with time

Your fiery touch upon my breast
filling me with
thoughts of love
forgetting
growing up was meant to be
a long trail of experiences in loving

Yet
that memory comes back now
more often than before
wondering if we left more than
just your sandals on the beach that night
maybe
something of each other
something
we meant to save for empty times
like these

Give Me One-Night Stands

You must know
by knowing me
I will be loved
if not by you,
then by someone

Even a one-night stand
has more to offer
than I find within
your arms
A little love—no pain
A little need—no shame
A little human awareness
Needing no apologies

A one-night stand
offers warmth
without broken promises
offers laughter
without cruel jokes
offers freedom in the
morning without heartache

But one night is not
enough for
you to disrobe
For the costumes you
wear are many and
complicated

One day you'll stand naked
before someone
with more and varied garb
Only to regret the warm
beds you've left
And I'll see you
shiver with the irony
of your plight.

Given Time

Given time
You'll come to see
That honesty
Will set you free.
And if you don't have time
My love
Best ask for mercy from above.

Real Life

Real Life is not
a page you turn
or a book you put aside.

Real Life is about
a heart that yearns
or a love that cannot hide.

Call Back

Just to hear your voice again
Even if only on the phone
Sets my soul on fire

There's something in your voice
That speaks to me, to my heart,
And makes me weak in the knees.

The chemistry is there.
Too bad Einstein's gone.
He could have mixed the right blend
To send you running back to me,
At least for a while.

My afternoon is useless now
I can't think
Except for thoughts of you.
Sad—you can't think of me too.

Sometimes

Sometimes I'd like to walk with you
If only, for a while.
Sometimes I'd like to talk with you
And just enjoy your smile.

The world is such as busy place
We save no time for living.
Sometimes I'd like to slow the pace
And have more time for giving.

God gives us each a cross to bear
And we must grin and bear it.
Sometimes we need a friend to care
Sometimes we need to share it.

You Said What?

You speak to me of good times
But I can feel the bad—

You speak to me of happiness
But I can see the sad—

You talk to me of sunshine
I see the cloudy skies—

You fill your day with laughter
At night tears fill your eyes.

With emptiness around you
You fill your heart with love.

Just let God's arms surround you
As He watches from above.

He is love.

Evolving I

And if you really do know me
Will you still be my friend?
Or turn your back and walk away
Just like some of them.

If my heart cracks this outer shell
And tries to make a connection
Will your heart let me just be me
And not try to make a correction?

What is this thing we call a "friend"
Do they have to all "fit in"
Or if they DARE to keep their differences
Do they maybe just sit in?

FOR A TIME

At some point I may have to DISSolve
Instead!!

Wanting You or One Eighty

As you brush by
I catch my breath
And hope you didn't see
The passion pouring
From my chest
That you bring forth in me.

Your touch is like
A Breath of Love
Your smile is warm and pure.

And when you leave
There's nothing left
For me but to endure.

My heart strings play
A song for you
But you don't want to hear
How I would love to hold you close
And always have you near.

Our lives are on two different paths
How sad they couldn't blend
But then again this may not last
Who knows how this will end?

A Perfect Rose

As I placed
a perfect rose on the table
this morning
I thought of you
Knowing
it would take
the same course
I've seen you take

A promise of beauty
and enjoyment
But for so short
a time
Opening now as you
opened your world to me.
In doing so
becoming so very beautiful to me
only to wither and die
by tomorrow morning

The morning of our love
was perfect
But just like
this rose
It lasts
too short a time

I think this rose has thorns
to remind lovers
and Me
of the sudden pain
Beauty
and dying love
can bring to a loving heart.

Daisies are safer
Plain, but no thorns

I'll plant daisies where
the rose bush grows!

Too Soon

It should have been you
who said Goodbye
not me
for I hadn't finished saying Hello

You see
I had much more to say
to show you
to tell you of my life.

My past gone from me now—yet—
bits and pieces show up
from time to time.

My present
boring at times
still
meaningful
at times like these
knowing
I've touched someone's heart
if only for a moment
and they've touched mine

My dreams
left open now to change
for they included you

I'm the one
that made the move
spoke too soon
spoke of Somethings that's
never entered my dreams of you.

Goodbye is such a
final act!

Let's say HELLO Again!

There's Always Hope

To feel so much
yet know so little
of life
Too Bad
Your sensuous, emotional,
and sheerly musical planes
can't get together
at least for a time

Imagine
the awakening you'd kindle
people like you
put on the wood pile
and only the shavings
used
used
to kindle the fire
that will burn through
the ages
only to come up
with ashes on your nose

The story of your
life is almost like mine
only difference
your fire went out

I went electric.

Section Two

Trying to Show an Inner Talent

(or Getting Off the Subject)

I scratch out these words hoping to show some feeling,
some intelligence, for the world today, or its happenings.

Plugging along, hoping to move some mountain one
day;
(if I could just get to its Valley).
Every day is an uphill climb, every now and then just
ease
back to that plateau of not caring. But,
when you say your prayers you have to care.

I pray for the hostages in Iran,
I pray for my adolescent child
fighting even greater fears than mine,
not knowing what to fear most.

A Father she's never known?
A Mother who's all love and understanding, but
no great strength?
Her peers who'll laugh or point a finger
if she doesn't turn out right?
The whole wide world,
changing so much every day?

But Hey!

Don't fear us!
Show us your guts!
Move ahead!
Show them it's not so bad!

A blueberry muffin and tea for breakfast,
A Karate lesson twice a week,
A job that takes your free time!
A striving for learning that makes
you fear your own drive … ?

Be Alive! Know that even out there,
life is just a cup of tea.
Maybe not for breakfast,
It depends if you want sugar, or lemon, or both,
Try always to flavor it with both,
the tartness makes the sweet mean so much more
and lasts so much longer.
You are not an ancient Egyptian scroll or painting,
Don't lie back and mold.
Shout! Shout today!
What you know and feel and feat!

Let us know you can bend and shape and change
this world as you learn.
You have to learn so much more than I did or at least
sooner.
Make it, my child, for no one can make it for you.
And you know what?
YOU WILL!!!

Please Be Dad

You settle yourself
in
with your life
forgetting
you gave her life

I understand
I'm glad
for
we had no life
that would complement
each other.

I compliment you
in what I've heard
But, sir,
you don't know
what you've missed

Don't ever feel bad
for love flows here
She loves you
for you are
DAD

Please, sir,
love her
She loves you
I've prayed for it
I've granted it

I've given it my OK
For you are OK
or
you were

Ask your new lady
not to worry
the only love
she wants here
in Florida
is DAD

Please, sir,
Be Dad
She needs it
Love Her Now!

On Rod McKuen
I Love Him

I love the writings of Rod McKuen
Because, they talk to you,
To the everyday Housewife.

He tells the things we all feel and
don't dare to tell.
He talks to the everyday person
or maybe not so everyday.

      because,

Maybe you are rich and unhappy,
maybe you are happy and unrich,
but still,
It will hit home like C&W music.
It will hit home so gently.
so meaningful, and yet so real,
Even a Multi-Millionaire has heard
his life story in these Verses.
Even a poor man has shouted for the feelings
piled on his chest
when he can't feel anymore, because life has dealt him
the wrong hand,
or maybe he just drew it.
That happens when we gamble too much.

So, if you don't want to gamble
just read Rod McKuen.
He tells it like it is,
or should be.
A little love,
A little pain,
an equal balance or
Pride and Shame.

Love him for he loves you
His words show it
in LOVE.

Millie

I remember you
You liked me
I loved you
You were Mama
I had none

You were all
hesitation
no recrimination
Just Love

Live and let live
You loved your kids
I loved You

I couldn't understand
the difference

A whole loaf of bread
a cigarette burn in
the furniture
still love

You're some lady
some mama
I borrowed you
You let me

I Love You

Annette

You are a friend of mine
We've known each other some long time
We've worked together
Played a little
But you and I always meet in the middle
Just stay the person that you are
You'll always be a shining star
Just glad to know you'll always be my friend

Nettie

Good friends
Are hard to come by
But some just settle in
Some stay awhile
Some come and go
Some never come again
But you will always be there
This I truly believe
You are one of the best of the lot
You'll never
Ever leave … me
Love,
Your friend,
Pat
April 8, 2014

Lisa

It was
A different rodeo
But we both had
A heck of a ride

Sometimes
We roped in the feelings
Sometimes
We just rode the pride

But here we are
Still standing
You with
The reins in your hands

Me with a new
Understanding
Of what must be
My life's plan

Love,
Your friend,
Pat

Linda, My Friend

A true friend is hard to find
One that's real and cool and kind
You have been there many years
You are one that I hold dear
Trust and honesty
Love and loyalty
These are your attributes
The tree of friendship
Grown so tall
With faith and love
At its roots

Love, Pat
April 8, 2014

Joy

You came across the water
And lay your hand upon a friend
Never Knowing at the time
Just how this thing would end
Life is just a journey
And we find joy there within
Who would know
That in this life
Joy
Would also be my friend
Love, Pat
March 29, 2014

Another Empty Monday

If Monday morning
comes up empty
just go on
just remember
there's another Friday night,
another Sunday afternoon

If you can make it through
the long week of
alarm clocks and coffee cups
and carpooling
You can search another
singles bar next weekend

You'll be
the hunter and the hunted
Your eyes will caress
the crowd
Searching for that certain smile
the all-knowing light
in someone's eyes
offering some warmth
some company
at least for a moment

Spending Sunday afternoon
napping
reading a new novel
and wondering how you
fell in love so fast
knowing it won't last

Another empty Monday
only heads you into Friday
with a smile
knowing
this week there'll be more

It's got to come up
Somewhere.

Autumn

Fall is here
the leaves have
turned their many
colors
The reds, greens, yellows,
and orange shades
light the dreary days
with their beauty

The splendor of nature
reaches its peak
Now
The whisper of blowing
leaves
dried and fallen
they crackle under your
feet
Such a beautiful
time of year
Autumn is Here!

Loss of a Child

I never thought
That you would leave
Before I had to go

I always thought
That you would grieve
But these things we can't know

God needed one
More angel so
He reached down from above

And chose you as
His special one
He selected you with love

He parts the heavens
With my prayer
And lets me see you
Resting there
Safe within
His strong but gentle arms

When I see footprints
On the beach
I kneel down
And slowly reach
To touch your gentle presence
Once again

My child
My best friend.

The Hunter

The Hunter
And the Hunted born

One seen noble
One with scorn

Wonder why
They seem forlorn?

Each one
Defiles the other

The Prayer

Lord
Take this other part of me
The part that no one else can see
And lay it somewhere deep within
Some little waif still free of sin
And when the sparrow comes along
To sing his same sweet soulful song
He'll tell the world
That I belong
As well as any other

My Child

A blessing from above
within my arms
A glance, and they don't
notice all your charms

But you will give me back
a hundredfold
more than all the diamonds
or the gold

I'll place my love within
your little heart
and you will give me
riches from the start

And as you grow
I'll be right here for you
Love,
from your mother
and your daddy too

No Longer

I am not
The person
In your memory

I am not
The person
You thought I should be

No longer a butterfly
Lost in the wind
More like a dolphin
That knows how to swim

So show me an ocean
And just set me free
I'll show you the person
I know I can be

Son

Wish I could go
To bat for you
Every time you stumble lightly—

Wish I could light
Each of your dark days
And make the sun shine brightly—

But as you grow
And become a man
These blocks you push behind you—

Will gently steer you
On your way
And maybe gently remind you—

That I am always
Here for you
I'll always be beside you—

And never fear to
Ask me, Son
If there's any way I can guide you—

But most of all
As you find your way
Remember
Above any other
You can always count
On one sure thing—

Love to you, Son,
From your mother.

This Sunny Morn

I look out
This sunny morn
O'er breaking waves
And beaches shorn

Power known
Not to this man
Or any other
On this land

Gentle power
From above
Filled with strength
Tho fraught with love

God, His strength,
And guiding hand
Shapes the earth
And molds the man

One thing man
Oft fails to see
The goal at hand
Spiritual destiny

On Miller Lites and Vantage Blues

With Miller Lites and Vantage Blues
you know you'll always pay your dues.
Your breath gets short,
your demeanor humble
(the latter might even let you stumble).
But this is everyday feelings for you,
don't let your muscles become like glue.

For feeling is so nice to know,
Even when you come up with nothing to show.
After 96 hours doing your share,
you might begin to believe that life isn't fair.
        But What Is?

Missing Pages of Life

As I see a page
from some book
blow down the street today
I have to wonder
if it's the page
from the book of life
that you must never
have read

Somehow
the part about
consideration of others' feelings
eluded you
I also remember a part
about
Human awareness
and being kind especially
to those who
Love You

I remember learning about
hearts being open
and honest about love
feeling good
and I always thought
the breath of love
was gentle with its
touch

Oh, well
maybe that was
before your time
or in a different school
of life
I wish you could go
back and reread the
part you've missed
It might change the
way you feel about
Some Things Today!

Save the Rest!

Who are you?
You
who can snatch a child
living
breathing
and so carelessly
lay it to rest in muddy waters

I feel
your mind
your heart
must have been muddied also
just as the river of death that
you have so willingly used
on little ones
not knowing of their end

Do they Know you?
So they trust you?
Do they walk beside you
and call you friend?

Let it end
this useless killing of
our children
Come forward now

PRAY
that what remains of your being
can be somehow cleansed by
HIM!!

Please
bury your sickness
with that last child
and
Save the rest!!

Abused One

Frightened child
In the dark
  Where's your sunshine
Where's your park

Who will show you
The clear blue sky
Who will hold you
That you won't cry

You'll know His love
Before long
His arms will hold you
Gentle but strong

You'll see the blue sky
From up above
You'll know His
Warm everlasting love

And as you gaze
At the clear blue sky
Father will sing you
Your lull-a-bye

Bella

You're not my little fella
but,
you're sweet as any little
man could be.

You're all feminine
and cozy
your cheeks are
oh,
so rosy
and I want to keep you
right here on my knee.

Section Three

Touch Me as You Tell Me

As you enter my room
and stroll to my bedside
that day.

Please
before the news
lay your warm hand
on my body.

Don't stand back.
Let me feel the warmth
of life flow,
as you tell me of what is to come.

Let me see in your eyes
the sincerity of
I'm sorry.
Squeeze my hand
as I say to you
Can't win 'em all!
And your reply
Nice to win a few.

At least I've won
this moment
the caring in your eyes
and in your touch
ease the pain.

Please
if you do care
lay your hand upon
my brow, make life valid;
and tell me now
with warmth and love.

For soon
I'll feel no more!

The pain I feel now,
or at least the pain of leaving
Too soon,
will leave quickly, If you
TOUCH ME AS YOU TELL ME!

If We Can, We Will, Friend

If I can fluff
one pillow
or straighten one sheet
to make your day
more comfortable or better
I will
For your smile
alone
brightens mine.

If I can lift
emotions high
by talk and laughter
to help you meet your new stress
I will
For your strength
has enriched my character
my being
in ways some would never understand.

If I can encourage
you
my friend
to not fear the cruelty
of ignorance
I will
for I know by dealing with it
it can't hurt
your beauty.

If you can know
in your heart
you have not really changed
then I can know in mine
there is a bright tomorrow
for all that really care!

A Lonely Man

Listen to the Silence
as it roars through Lonely Hearts.
Hear the tears slam to the Floor
as their worlds fall apart.

His Fingers trace the cool, damp glass.
The lines Rain left Behind
He rearranges Memories to
suit his Needs this Time.

You wonder if his Broken Dreams
Lie in some Quiet Wood
or along some Gentle Mountain Stream.
I'd Find Them
        If I Could—

Nurses' Nightmares

Oasis is no longer
A haven from the sun
Now it seems it's just a toy
That HCFA sees as fun

PPS is rampant
SCICs are flooding in
And Lord
What will I ever do
When RAPs start getting thin?

The budget's growing slimmer
The time's getting short
If Medicare
Won't play fair
It's no longer sport.

They come up with all this jargon
To blow a nurse's mind
Then tell her all the paperwork
Must be on time.

Home Health Nurses

Your home health nurse is calling
She's knocking at your door
She's come to fix your bandages
And medicine and more

She'll greet you with a smile
She'll leave you with a grin'
She'll find a neighbor or a friend
You'll begin to think is kin

There's never any mountain
She won't move for you
And if she needs to move you
She'll do that too

She'll contact your doctor
Or get you therapy
And if your staples must come out
She'll do all three

So seniors keep your hopes up
Don't let it be a scare
Your nurse will always find a way
To work with Medicare

PPS

With Medicare up on the hill
Changing rules
And signing bills

With PPS and SCIC and RAP
And all that other
"Red Tape" crap

I don't have to wonder
Why I go to work each day
The patient's smile my sunshine
Their gratitude my pay

The patients must eat cat food
With torn sheet bib
They sit with fancy napkins
And eat prime rib

Medicare "A" or "B"
No matter which part
They'll never stop a nurse
Who works from the heart

One day with open wounds
As they lay up in that bed
I hope the tape I carry
Isn't only red.